To my
Ivan,

wishing you life &
love, happiness &

joy in the next

phase of your life.

Love you Cian.

Ballygebuly 2th 2023

LIVE LIFE
to the full

A Helen Exley
QUOTATION COLLECTION

Helen Exley

ILLUSTRATED BY JULIETTE CLARKE
EDITED BY HELEN EXLEY

Published in 2018 as Live! Laugh! Love! by Helen Exley®
LONDON in Great Britain. This revised edition published in 202
Illustrated by Juliette Clarke ©Helen Exley Creative Ltd 2018, 202
Design and creation by Helen Exley © Helen Exley Creative Ltd 2018, 202
All the words by Pam Brown, Charlotte Gray, Pamela Dugdale,
Stuart&Linda Macfarlane and Pamela Brown are copyright
© Helen Exley Creative Ltd 2018, 2021.

ISBN 978-1-78485-321-1

12 11 10 9 8 7 6 5 4 3 2 1

OTHER BOOKS IN THE SERIES

BELIEVE IN YOURSELF   THE RESILIENCE BOOK   FOREVER TOGETHE
CALM AND MINDFULNESS   THE BOOK OF POSITIVE THOUGHTS

Helen Exley®LONDON
16 Chalk Hill, Watford, Hertfordshire, WD19 4BG, UK
www.helenexley.com

LIVE LIFE
to the full

A Helen Exley
QUOTATION COLLECTION

*E*nthusiasm is everything. It must be taut and vibrating like a guitar string.

PELÉ, B. 1940

…there are times when I think to myself how wonderful life can be! Believe me, it's true! So stop what you're doing this minute and get happy. Work at making yourself happy!

HARUKI MURAKAMI, B. 1949

I have lost much - but I have life.
I will live it to the full.
And make every second count, knowing that it has been the greatest gift of all.

CHARLOTTE GRAY

*Every day
brings a chance
for you to draw in
a breath,
kick off your shoes,
and dance.*

OPRAH WINFREY, B. 1954

The moment when you first wake up in the morning is the most wonderful of the twenty-four hours. No matter how weary or dreary you may feel, you possess the certainty that, during the day that lies before you, absolutely anything may happen. And the fact that it practically always doesn't, matters not a jot. The possibility is always there.

MONICA BALDWIN

Laugh your heart out.

Dance in the rain.

Cherish the moment.

Ignore the pain.

Live, Laugh, Love.

Forgive and Forget.

Life's too short to be

Living with regrets…

AUTHOR UNKNOWN

Life is a great big
canvas;
throw all the paint
on it you can.

DANNY KAYE (1913-1987)

*Laughing
cheerfulness
throws sunlight
on all the paths
of life.*

JEAN PAUL RICHTER (1763-1825)

*From wonder
into wonder
existence opens.*

LAO TZU (604 B.C.-531 B.C.)

For me life is swimming in an ocean of gratitude, love, joy, humor, wonder, curiosity, passion, hope and creativity, and never finding the shore.

HUNTER "PATCH" ADAMS, B. 1945

$\mathcal{Y}$ou must learn day by day, year by year, to broaden your horizon. The more things you love, the more you are interested in, the more you enjoy, the more you are indignant about – the more you have left when anything happens.

ETHEL BARRYMORE (1879-1959)

Happiness does not come boxed and labelled.
Cannot be supplied by manufacturers.
Grows wild.
Is all about you.
Free.

PAM BROWN (1928-2014)

Life is so fragile
it is outrageous
not to be happy.

PHYLLIDA LAW, B.1932

Hope is only th

Most of us miss out on life's big prizes. The Pulitzer, the Nobel, Oscars, Emmys, Grammys. But we are all eligible for life's smallest pleasures. A pat on the back. A kiss behind the ear. A four-pound barramundi. A full moon. An empty parking space. A crackling fire. A great meal. A glorious sunset. Hot soup. Cold beer. A laugh with your mates. Don't fret about getting life's grand awards. Enjoy its tiny delights. There are plenty there for all of us.

AUTHOR UNKNOWN

...ove of life.

HENRI FRÉDÉRIC AMIEL (1821-1881)

Life is fun

Life is happiness

Life is gladness

Life is loving

Life is helping

Life is gentleness

Life is laughter

Oh life is beautiful.

ALLISON HUDDART, AGE 10

*I*n the morning, how good it is to see the brilliant light of the blessed summer day, always brightest just after rain, and to see how every tree and plant is full of new life and abounding gladness; and to feel one's own thankfulness of heart, and that it is good to live...

GERTRUDE JEKYLL (1843-1932)

Blooming under a cold moon, we are like fireworks... Rising, shining, and finally scattering and fading. So until that moment comes when we vanish like fireworks... Let us sparkle brightly, Always...

TITE KUBO, B. 1977

Laughter
is the
joyous
universal
evergreen
of life.

ABRAHAM LINCOLN (1809-1865)

There's so much fun to be had in life that there could never be enough time to cram it all in.

STUART & LINDA MACFARLANE

The first thing to be done is laughter, because that sets the trend for the whole day.

OSHO (1931-1990)

Each day comes bearing its own gifts. Untie the ribbons.

RUTH ANN SCHABACKER

I like nonsense, it wakes up the brain cells.
Fantasy is a necessary ingredient in living.
It's a way of looking at life through the wrong
end of a telescope. Which is what I do. And
that enables you to laugh at life's realities.

DR. SEUSS (1904-1991)

*Life –
the most wonderful
fairground attraction
of all –
enjoy the ride.*

STUART & LINDA MACFARLANE

Happiness is love bubbling forth into the newness and fullness of true life. When we are happy, we move forward. We dive deep within. We fly.

SRI CHINMOY (1931-2007)

A day without laught

a day wasted.

CHARLIE CHAPLIN (1889-1997)

My secret joy is found late at night when a million stars are reflected in the still surface of the lake. I paddle out, slip down to lie on my back in the bottom of the canoe, and drift on the water in the silence, held by a million points of light above and below, my heart breaking with the joy of being alive on this beautiful planet.

ORIAH MOUNTAIN DREAMER

*L*ive your truth.
Express your love.
Share your enthusiasm.
Take action towards your dreams.
Walk your talk.
Dance and sing to your music.
Embrace your blessings.
Make today worth remembering.

STEVE MARABOLI, B. 1975

Each day is a gift.
Open it.
Celebrate.
Enjoy it.

STUART & LINDA MACFARLANE

*F*un is the most conservative element of society, and it ought to be cherished and encouraged by all lawful means. People never plot mischief when they are merry. Laughter is an enemy to malice, a foe to scandal and a friend to every virtue.
It promotes good temper, enlivens the heart and brightens the intellect.

MARK ADELER

There is only one world, the world pressing against you at this minute. There is only one minute in which you are alive, this one. Happiness is not a goal dependent on some future event, it could be with us all the time if we only made the effort to recognise it. And surely the best way to live is by accepting each minute as an unrepeatable miracle. Which is exactly what it is.

ROY BOLITHO

Fill each day.
Give it your youth,
your health,
your abilities,
your hope
– so that your whole life
will be a wonder.
And your memories sweet.

PAM BROWN (1928-2014)

*T*here is beauty around us, in things large and small, in friends, family, the countryside, a singing bird. Stop to reflect, to give thanks, to contemplate the gift of another day. Touch the wonders of life and rejoice.

ANTON CHEKHOV (1860-1904)

Today a new sun rises for me; everything lives, everything is animated, everything seems to speak to me of my passion, everything invites me to cherish it…

NINON DE L'ENCLOS (1620-1705)

You have your brush,
you have your colours,
you paint paradise,
then in you go.

NIKOS KAZANTZAKIS (1883-1957)

Give every day
the chance to become
the most beautiful of your life.

MARK TWAIN (1835-1910)

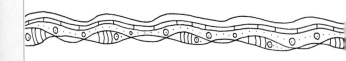

*T*oday's mission:
To be so busy loving life
that I have no time for drama,
regret, hate, worry, or fear.

KAREN SALMANSOHN

A life is only rich
if you fill it with experiences.

PELÉ, B. 1940

Joy is an ocean –
we can scoop it up by the bucketful
and there will always be plenty more.

STUART & LINDA MACFARLANE

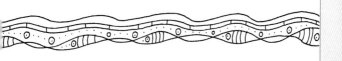

*T*he aim of life is to live, and to live means to be aware, joyously, drunkenly, serenely, divinely aware.

HENRY MILLER (1891-1980)

Wake up

and live.

BOB MARLEY (1945-1981)

*T*he thing-in-itself, the will-to-live, exists whole
and undivided in every being, even in the
tiniest; it is present as completely as in all that
ever were, are, and will be, taken together.

ARTHUR SCHOPENHAUER (1788-1860)

*E*verything is extraordinarily clear. I see the whole landscape before me, I see my hands, my feet, my toes, and I smell the rich river mud. I feel a sense of tremendous strangeness and wonder at being alive. Wonder of wonders.

GAUTAMA BUDDHA (c.563 B.C. - 483 B.C.)

Life is just a bowl of cherries, so live and laugh and laugh at love, love a laugh, laugh and love.

BOB FOSSE (1927-1987)

Love is plant of tenderest growth: treat it well, take thought for it and it may grow strong and perfume your whole life.

FRANK HARRIS (1856-1931)

"Just living is not enough,"
said the butterfly.
"One must have sunshine,
freedom,
and a little flower."

HANS CHRISTIAN ANDERSEN (1805-1875)

*C*lose your eyes.

You might try saying…

something like this:

"The sun is shining overhead.

The sky is blue and sparkling.

Nature is calm and in control

of the world –

and I, as nature's child,

am in tune

with the Universe."

DALE CARNEGIE (1888-1955)

This is the gift you
have been given
- a world of wonders.
Enough to delight
a thousand,
thousand lives.
And it is yours.

PAMELA DUGDALE

*L*et us not therefore go hurrying
about and collecting honey,
bee-like, buzzing here and there
impatiently from a knowledge
of what is to be arrived at.
But let us open out like leaves
of a flower, and be passive
and receptive: budding patiently
under the eye of Apollo
and taking hints from
every noble insect
that favours us with a visit.

JOHN KEATS (1795-1821)

The weather forecast says
"Rain! Rain! Rain!"
but your heart says
"Sun! Sun! Sun!"

STUART & LINDA MACFARLANE

*S*tep into the unknown – live in it – and be prepared to hang out there. We cannot know what's in store for us, and by hanging on to what's familiar we block the new. Until hanging on by our fingertips to the old life, fed up with prising off our fingertips one by one, it simply kicks us into the abyss. As we fall screaming, it prepares a feather mattress for us. Stunned, we wonder why we didn't dive off to begin with. Live life. There's no waiting game. What is it you want to create right now? How do you want to be?
Do it now.

CARON KEATING (1962-2004)

DANCE,
my heart;
O dance
today
with joy!

KABIR (1380-1420)

I would rather be ashes than dust, I would rather that my spark should burn out in a brilliant blaze than it should be stifled by dry rot. I would rather be a superb meteor, every atom in me in magnificent glow, than a sleepy and permanent planet.

JACK LONDON (1876-1916)

"Life," he said, and he was always urging this on Muriel in one form or another, "life is beautiful, so long as it is consuming you. When it is rushing through you, destroying you, life is glorious. It is best to roar away, like a fire with a great draught, white-hot to the last bit".

D. H. LAWRENCE (1885-1930)

*T*ell me,
what is it you plan
to do with your one wild
and precious life?

MARY OLIVER (1935-2019)

*U*se your eyes as if tomorrow you would be stricken blind... Hear the music of voices, the song of the bird, the mighty strains of an orchestra, as if you would be stricken deaf tomorrow. Touch each object as if tomorrow your tactile sense would fail. Smell the perfume of the flowers, taste with relish each morsel, as if tomorrow you could never smell and taste again. Make the most of every sense; glory in all the facets of pleasure and beauty which the world reveals to you.

HELEN KELLER (BORN BOTH DEAF AND BLIND) (1880-1968)

*H*ave fun! Enjoy!
Open your arms
to all flowers and music,
every lovely thing.
Bold adventure
and astonishment.
Love. Be brave. Be curious.
Be courteous.
Discover a wider world.

CHARLOTTE GRAY

To awaken each morning with a smile brightening my face; to greet the day with reverence for the opportunities it contains; to approach my work with a clean mind; to hold ever before me, even in the doing of little things, the ultimate purpose toward which I am working; to meet men and women with laughter on my lips and love in my heart; to be gentle, kind, and courteous through all the hours; to approach the night with weariness that ever woos sleep and the joy that comes from work well done – this is how I desire to waste wisely my days.

THOMAS DEKKER (c.1570-1632)

Joy irradiates the world.

PAMELA DUGDALE

What is Life?
It is the flash of a firefly
in the night.
It is the breath of a buffalo
in the winter time.
It is the little shadow
which runs across the grass
and loses itself in the sunset.

CROWFOOT, BLACKFOOT INDIAN LEADER

s life?

*I*f we had keen vision of all
that is ordinary in human life,
it would be like hearing
the grass grow
or the squirrel's heartbeat,
and we should die
of that roar which is
the other side of silence.

GEORGE ELIOT (MARY ANN EVANS) (1819-1880)

*H*ere we are,
specks on a planet, miniscule beside our sun.
A sun lost in the countless suns of our small
galaxy, – our lives pass in a flickering of time
and yet for that brief moment
we are rich beyond imagination.
Our senses reel in wonder.
Fire and rivers, mountains, forests, flowers.
Creatures of every kind, from ant to whale,
from diatoms to tigers.
And we have the power to weave all that we
know into new forms, new music,
new perception.
We have the gifts of love and laughter.

PAMELA DUGDALE

*Keep a green tree
in your heart and perhaps
a singing bird will come.*

CHINESE PROVERB

No more brooding,
No more despondency.
Your life will become
The beauty of a rose,
The song of the dawn,
The dance of twilight.

SRI CHINMOY (1931-2007)

There are only two ways to
live your life.
One is as though nothing
is a miracle.
The other is as though
everything is a miracle.

ALBERT EINSTEIN (1879-1955)

*E*ach time
for the first time.
Each moment
the only moment.

JON KABAT-ZINN, B. 1944

*L*ive all you can;

it's a mistake not to.

It doesn't so much matter

what you do in particular

so long as you have your life.

If you haven't had that,

what have you had?

HENRY JAMES (1843-1916)

A smile starts on the lips,
A grin spreads to the eyes,
A chuckle comes from the belly;
But a good laugh
bursts forth from the soul,
Overflows,
and bubbles all around.

CAROLYN BIRMINGHAM

I wish you laughter.
Spluttering laughter,
whooping laughter,
the helpless silent laughter
that sends you to the floor in tears.
Giggling laughter, heads together.
The shared laughter in the
dark of an auditorium.
The laughter that crowns success,
that springs from joy.
Kind laughter,
laughter that reaches out and
gathers others to itself.
And never mind who stares.

PAM BROWN (1928-2014)

*M*ay the wind

be gentle

May the waves

be calm

May the elements

smile on all our wishes.

WOLFGANG AMADEUS MOZART
(1756-1791)

*W*hen you arise
in the morning
think of
what a privilege it is
to be alive,
to think,
to enjoy,
to love...

MARCUS AURELIUS (A.D. 121 - 180)

We live closely.
We live happily.
We laugh together.
We laugh at all.
We love fun.
We love jokes.
We love sharing.
We love caring.
We love life very much.
We live.
We laugh.
We love.

AUTHOR UNKNOWN

...I know nothing else but miracles...
To me every hour of the light
and dark is a miracle,
Every cubic inch of space
is a miracle,
Every square yard of the surface
of the earth is spread
with the same,
Every foot of the interior
swarms with the same.

WALT WHITMAN (1819-1892)

Tomorrow is the most important thing in life.
Comes into us at midnight very clean. It's
perfect when it arrives and it puts itself in our
hands. It hopes we've learned something from
yesterday.

JOHN WAYNE (1907-1979)

Every day's a kick!

OPRAH WINFREY, B. 1954

*D*on't evaluate your life in terms of achievements, trivial or monumental, along the way... Instead, wake up and appreciate everything you encounter along the path. Enjoy the flowers that are there for your pleasure. Tune in to the sunrise, the little children, the laughter, the rain, and the birds. Drink it all in... there is no way to happiness; happiness is the way.

DR. WAYNE W. DYER (1940 -2015)

happines

s the way

*L*ife is an opportunity, benefit from it.

Life is beauty, admire it.

Life is bliss, taste it.

Life is a dream, realize it.

Life is a challenge, meet it.

Life is a duty, complete it.

Life is a game, play it.

Life is a promise, fulfil it.

Life is a sorrow, overcome it

Life is a song, sing it.

Life is a struggle, accept it.

Life is a tragedy, confront it.

Life is an adventure, dare it.

Life is luck, make it.

Life is too precious, do not destroy it.

Life is life, fight for it.

MOTHER TERESA (1910-1997)

The best and sweetest
things in life are things
you cannot buy:
the music of the birds at dawn,
the rainbow in the sky.
The dazzling magic
of the stars,
the miracle of light.

PATIENCE STRONG (1907-1990)

Live Loud,
Love Loud,
Laugh Loud,
Play Loud,
Cry Loud –
Isn't that
what life's about!

SAMUEL NAZER WALSH

Another fresh new year is here…
Another year to live! To banish worry,
doubt, and fear,
To love and laugh and give!
This bright new year is given me
To live each day with zest...
To daily grow and try to be
My highest and my best!
I have the opportunity once more to right
some wrongs, To pray for peace, to plant
a tree.
And sing more joyful songs!

WILLIAM ARTHUR WARD (1921-1994)

May you live
all the days
of your life.

JONATHAN SWIFT (1667-1745)

Do not say,
"It is morning," and dismiss it
with a name of yesterday.
See it for the first time
as a newborn child
that has no name.

RABINDRANATH TAGORE (1861-1941)

*I*f I had my life to live over...
I'd dare to make more mistakes next time.
I'd relax. I would limber up.
I would be sillier than I have been this trip.
I would take fewer things seriously.
I would take more chances.
I would take more trips.
I would climb more mountains and swim
more rivers.
I would eat more ice creams and less beans.
I would perhaps have more actual troubles,
But I'd have fewer imaginary ones.

NADINE STAIR

*T*here is just one way to make sure of immortality, and that is to love this life and live it as richly and helpfully as we can.

HELEN KELLER (BORN BOTH DEAF AND BLIND) (1880-1968)

Laugh a lot, love

ot, live forever.

STUART & LINDA MACFARLANE

*N*o matter how dire the circumstances, there always comes a point when you can have a laugh and forget about what's happening for a minute – realise you are still alive and all things are possible.

CARON KEATING (1962-2004)

Dear Human:

...You came here to learn personal love.

Universal love.

Messy love. Sweaty Love.

Crazy love. Broken love.

Whole love. Infused with divinity.

Lived through the grace of stumbling.

Demonstrated through the beauty of...

messing up.

Often.

You didn't come here to be perfect, you already are.

You came here to be gorgeously human.

Flawed and fabulous.

And rising again into remembering.
But unconditional love? Stop telling that story.
Love in truth doesn't need any adjectives.
It doesn't require modifiers.
It doesn't require the condition of perfection.
It only asks you to show up.
And do your best.
That you stay present and feel fully.
That you shine and fly and laugh and cry and
hurt and heal and fall and get back up and play
and work and live and die as YOU.
Its enough.
It's Plenty.

COURTNEY A. WALSH

*L*ive life fully while you're here. Experience everything. Take care of yourself and your friends. Have fun, be crazy, be weird. Go out and screw up! You're going to anyway, so you might as well enjoy the process. Take the opportunity to learn from your mistakes: find the cause of your problem and eliminate it. Don't try to be perfect; just be an excellent example of being human.

ANTHONY ROBBINS

Laugh and be merry together... Glad till the dancing stops, and the lilt of the music ends. Laugh till the game is played; and be you merry my friends.

JOHN MASEFIELD (1878-1967)

*Work like you don't
need the money,
love like your
heart has never been broken,
and dance
like no one is watching.*

LARRY MCMURTRY, B. 1936

The earth laughs in flowers.

RALPH WALDO EMERSON
(1803-1882)

Our world is unbelievably beautiful and alive. I will never tire of observing it, nor will I ever cease to be moved by a sublime landscape, the texture of a rock, and the power of the elements that formed them. I will always be filled with wonder at the magic of lightning, the delicacy of tiny flowers, glowing lichens, curious animals, and fascinating people. This beauty nourishes me, and it is more important as a source of energy than any of the delicious food I eat.

ANNE COLLET

*T*o fill the hour – that is happiness; to fill the hour, and leave no crevice for a repentance or an approval.

RALPH WALDO EMERSON (1803-1882)

If there's one thing I learned, it's that nobody is here forever. You have to live for the moment, each and every day... the here, the now.

SIMONE ELKELESS, B. 1970

It's the little sparks of happiness that light up a life.

PAMELA DUGDALE

*L*augh as much as you breathe
and love as long as you live.

ANDREA LEVY, B. 1956

With mirth and laughter let old wrinkles
come.

WILLIAM SHAKESPEARE (1564-1616)

As soon as you have made a thought,
laugh at it.

LAO TZU (604 B.C.-531 B.C.)

Ten thousand flowers in spring,

the moon in autumn,

a cool breeze in summer,

snow in winter.

If your mind isn't clouded by

unnecessary things,

this is the best season of your life.

WU-MEN (1183-1260)

We get one go this side of eternity, one go! It's not a dress rehearsal, it's one go and you make the most of it and you take opportunities that come along that you like and you go for it.

ANN WIDDECOMBE, B. 1947

The sun and stars that float in the open air... the apple-shaped Earth and we upon it... surely the drift of them is something grand; I do not know what it is except that it is grand, and that it is happiness...

WALT WHITMAN (1819-1892)

Life
itself
is the
proper
binge.

JULIA CHILD (1912-2004)

*S*he worked her toes into the sand,
feeling the tiny delicious pain
of the friction of tiny chips of silicon
against the tender flesh between her toes.
That's life. It hurts,
it's dirty, and it feels very, very good.

ORSEN SCOTT CARD, B. 1951

We should never
be so busy that we miss out
on the sheer wonder
of being alive.

EMILY DICKINSON (1830-1886)

Begin doing
what you want to do now.
We have only
this moment,
sparkling like a star
in our hand
and melting
like a snowflake.

SIR FRANCIS BACON (1561-1626)

*W*hat is the bedrock on which we can stand, despite the essentially inconclusive nature of life? Love, hope, awareness of the moment, the exquisite joy of simply being alive...

STEPHEN BOWKETT

Life is fast flowing like a river. The day that is gone can never come back. So make the best use of your time. Crying out "Alas! Alas!" at the last moment will be of no avail.

SWAMI BRAHMANANDA (1863-1922)

*H*appiness
is a quiet,
perpetual rejoicing
in small events.

PAM BROWN (1928-2014)

If you get the choice
of sitting it out and looking at life,
or dancing your way through it,
I hope you dance!

FR. BRIAN D'ARCY, B. 1945

When you allow yourself to trust joy
and embrace it,
you will find you dance with everything.

EMMANUEL

Wear your dreams like diamonds.

STUART & LINDA MACFARLANE

*L*ive your Joy,
Let nature's curious wisdom fill you.
Let the world's heritage guide you.
Paint your canvases,
play your tunes.

SIR THOMAS MORE (1478-1535)

When I feel so happy
I jump to touch the sky,
When I feel so happy
I climb a mountainside,
When I feel so happy
I run around the world.

ANDREW MOSS, AGE 10

There is a vitality, a life force, an energy,
a quickening that is translated through you
into action and because there is only one of
you in all time, this expression is unique.
And if you block it, it will never exist through
any other medium and be lost, the world
will not have it.

MARTHA GRAHAM (1894-1991)

Of all the gifts that one could imagine,
I cannot think of a greater one than life itself.

STANLEY KUNITZ (1905-2006)

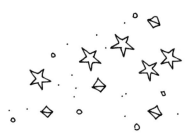

Without enthusiasm life becomes a dry and tasteless experience. Anyone can become enthusiastic for a little while but to keep enthusiasm steadily flowing through our life is a great art. However, the secret is remarkably simple: live in a state of appreciation; appreciate the special qualities within everyone; appreciate the wonder of nature and give thanks to the cycle of life and everyone's contribution to it. Enthusiasm is infectious, especially when it is based on an appreciation of, and love for, life itself.

DADI JANKI (1916-2020)

Happiness is riding
Happiness is free
Happiness is jumping
So it must be me!

ANDREW TROWBRIDGE, AGE 7

*W*hether seventy or sixteen,
there is in every being's heart
a love of wonder;
the sweet amazement at the stars
and starlike things and thoughts;
the undaunted challenge of events,
the unfailing childlike appetite
for what comes next,
and the joy in the game of life.

SAMUEL ULLMAN (1840-1924)

The sound of laughter
has always seemed to me
the most civilized
music in the universe.

SIR PETER USTINOV (1921-2004)

A good, real, unrestrained, hearty laugh is a sort of glorified internal massage, performed rapidly and automatically. It manipulates and revitalizes corners and unexplored crannies of the system that are unresponsive to most other exercise methods.

MAUD VAN BUREN, IN "NEW YORK TRIBUNE"

Let us go singing as far as we go: the road will be less tedious.

VIRGIL (70 B.C.-19 B.C.)

The incredible gift of the ordinary! Glory comes streaming from the table of daily life.

MACRINA WIEDERKEHR

The most visible creators I know of are those artists whose medium is life itself. The ones who express the inexpressible – without brush, hammer, clay, or guitar. They neither paint nor sculpt – their medium is being. Whatever their presence touches has increased life. They see and don't have to draw. They are the artists of being alive.

J. STONE

Joys are

our wings.

EAN PAUL RICHTER (1763-1825)

..adventures, they're fun, but the real adventure
s every single day when you wake up, wiggle
our toes and think "Ooh a new day". And you
ever know what will happen.

OSIE SWALE POPE, B. 1946

Make voyages!
Attempt them!
There's nothing else...

TENNESSEE WILLIAMS (1911-1983)

I wish I knew what people meant
when they say they find "emptiness"
in this wonderful adventure of living,
which seems to me to pile up its glories
like an horizon-wide sunset
as the light declines. I'm afraid
I'm an incorrigible life-lover,
life-wanderer, and adventurer.

EDITH WHARTON (1862-1937)

*L*ife is the best thing ever, and we have no business taking it for granted. It is so easy to waste our lives, to take for granted the way the melody in a symphony rises and falls and disappears and rises again.

Get a real life, not a pursuit of the next promotion, the bigger pay-cheque, the larger house. Get a life in which you notice the smell of salt water pushing itself on a breeze, a life in which you stop and watch how a red-tailed hawk circles over the water, or the way a baby scowls with concentration when she tries to pick up a sweet with her thumb and first finger.

ANNA QUINDLEN, B. 1953

*L*eave home in the sunshine:
Dance through a meadow –
Or sit by a stream and just be.
The lilt of the water
Will gather your worries
And carry them down to the sea.

J. DONALD WALTERS (1926-2013)

Set wide the window

et me drink the day.

EDITH WHARTON (1862-1937)

*T*here is nothing more wonderful than the astonishing fact that we are alive, that we breathe, eat, sleep, walk, laugh, cry.

ALAN WATTS (1915-1973)

The same stream of life that runs through my veins night and day runs through the world and dances in rhythmic measures.

It is the same life that shoots in joy, through the dust of the earth in numberless blades of grass and breaks into tumultuous waves of leaves and flowers.

RABINDRANATH TAGORE (1861-1941)

Every day is a birth day;
every moment
of it is new to us;
we are born again,
renewed for fresh work
and endeavour.

ISAAC WATTS (1674-1748)

Find out where joy resides,
and give it a voice
far beyond singing.
For to miss the joy
is to miss all.

ROBERT LOUIS STEVENSON (1850-1894)

*C*herish your solitude.
Take trains by yourself to places you have never been. Sleep out alone under the stars. Learn how to drive a stick shift. Go so far away that you stop being afraid of not coming back. Say no when you don't want to do something. Say yes if your instincts are strong, even if everyone around you disagrees. Decide whether you want to be liked or admired. Decide if fitting in is more important than finding out what you're doing here. Believe in kissing.

EVE ENSLER, B. 1953

*I expand and live
in the warm day
like corn and melons.*

RALPH WALDO EMERSON (1803-1882)

Don't hurry, don't worry. You're only here for a short visit. So be sure to stop and smell the flowers.

WALTER HAGEN (1892-1969)

The fall
of a leaf
is a whisper
to the living.

RUSSIAN PROVERB

*T*o be sensual… is to respect and rejoice in the face of life, of life itself, and to be present in all that one does, from the effort of living to the breaking of bread.

JAMES BALDWIN (1924-1987)

Joy in one's heart and some laughter on one's lips is a sign that the person down deep has a pretty good grasp of life.

HUGH SIDEY (1927-2005)

Spend all you have for loveliness,
Buy it and never count the cost…
And for a breath of ecstasy
Give all that you have been, or could be.

SARA TEASDALE (1884-1933)

*E*ach moment of the year has its own beauty, a picture which was never seen before and which shall never be seen again.

RALPH WALDO EMERSON (1803-1882)

Life is not measured by the number of breaths we take, but by the great moments which take our breath away.

FROM "THE FRIENDSHIP BOOK OF FRANCIS GAY"

Is it so small a thing to have enjoyed the sun, to have lived light in the spring, to have loved, to have thought, to have done?

MATTHEW ARNOLD (1822-1888)

I feel glad
as the ponies do
when the fresh green grass
starts in the beginning
of the year.

TEN BEARS, YAMPARETHKA COMANCHE CHIEF

And remember this: every time we laugh, we take a kink out of the chain of life.

JOSH BILLINGS (1818-1885)

I gather up
all the little things
that have astonished
and enchanted me.
They crown my days
in a diadem of joy.

PAM BROWN (1928-2014)

Dance first.
Think later.

SAMUEL BECKETT (1906-1989)

Do anything, bu

There's joy all around us!
Why wait till tomorrow?
We've only this moment to live.
A heaven within us
Is ours for the finding,
A freedom no riches can give!

J. DONALD WALTERS (1926-2013)

et it produce joy.

WALT WHITMAN (1819-1892)

Live in each season as it passes, breathe
the air, drink the drink, taste the fruit…

HENRY DAVID THOREAU (1817-1862)

I look up - and laugh - and love - and lift.

HOWARD ARNOLD WALTER (1883-1918)

The human race
has only one really effective weapon
and that is laughter.
Against the assault of laughter
nothing can stand.

MARK TWAIN (1835-1910)

$\mathcal{Y}$ou must live in the present,
launch yourself on every wave,
find your eternity in each moment.
Fools stand on their island
of opportunities
and look toward another land.
There is no other land;
there is no other life
but this.

HENRY DAVID THOREAU (1817-1862)

Take time to be friendly –

It is the road to happiness.

Take time to dream –

It is hitching your wagon to a star.

Take time to love and to be loved –

It is the privilege of the gods.

Take time to laugh –

It is the music of the soul.

FROM AN OLD ENGLISH SAMPLER

The purpose of life,
after all, is to live it,
to taste experience
to the utmost,
to reach out eagerly
and without fear
for newer and richer
experience.

ELEANOR ROOSEVELT (1884-1962)

to dream

*W*e creatures have only existed for
two million years
– a late comer to this earth,
this little planet held in a solar system
of only twelve billion years of life.
Such vast numbers are lost among
a cloud of suns of unimaginable extent.
And yet in a flicker of time
we have moved from ignorance
to bewildering discovery.

A speck of sand at the edges of a small galaxy

- yet beautiful beyond belief,

peopled by creatures who search for wisdom,

who think and learn and change,

creating wonders.

To be alive,

to see, to hear, to speak, to love.

Value every second of existence.

You are a miracle.

PAM BROWN (1928-2014)

Happiness, happiness, you touched my small head.

KEMA AKOMA-MORDI, AGE 10

*I*nto each day,
put in about one teaspoonful of
good spirits, a dash of fun,
a pinch of folly, a sprinkling of play
and a heaping cupful
of good humour.

AUTHOR UNKNOWN

Happiness is going to parties,
eating lots and lots of food
and making yourself fat and chubby
and instead of running
you bounce all the way home.

JANET BARTON, AGE 8

To a young hear

*L*et go the sad times,

hold on to the glad times,

the picnics and parties and fun,

the tingle and glow of

a walk in the snow,

the lazy days sprawled in the sun.

PAMELA DUGDALE

verything is fun.

CHARLES DICKENS (1812-1870)

*Music in the soul
can be heard
by the universe.*

LAO TZU (604 B.C.-531 B.C.)

Happiness,
not in another place
but this place...
not for another hour,
but this hour.

WALT WHITMAN (1819-1892)

You have to
sniff out joy,
keep your nose
to the joy-trail.

BUFFY SAINTE-MARIE, B. 1941

A child's hand rests in yours.
A bird sings.
A dragon-fly gleams above the lake.
A star falls.
Any sorrow is a little price to pay
for this great wonder.

PAMELA DUGDALE

To see a World in a Grain of Sand,
And a Heaven in a Wild Flower,
Hold infinity in the palm of your hand
and Eternity in an hour.

WILLIAM BLAKE (1757-1827)

I struggle to live for the beauty of a pansy,

for a little black baby's song,

for my lover's laugh.

I struggle for the blaze of pink

across the evening sky...

I struggle for life and the pursuit of its

happiness.

I struggle to fill my house with joy.

STEPHANIE BYRD

Life
is ours to
be spent...

D. H. LAWRENCE (1885-1930)

*I*t is fabulously fantastic to be alive.

STUART & LINDA MACFARLANE

Life is in the living,
in the tissue of every day and hour.

STEPHEN LEACOCK (1869-1944)

If you ask me
what I came into
this life to do,
I will tell you:
I came to live out loud.

EMILE ZOLA (1840-1902)

*J*oin the whole of creation of animate things in a deep, heartfelt joy that you are alive; that you see the sun, that you are in this glorious earth which nature has made so beautiful and which is yours to enjoy.

DR. WILLIAM OSLER (1849-1919)

We should consider every day lost on which we have not danced at least once. And we should call every truth false which was not accompanied by at least one laugh.

FRIEDRICH WILHELM NIETZSCHE (1844-1900)

*To live is so startling
it leaves little time
for anything else.*

EMILY DICKINSON (1830-1886)

*I*t began in mystery,
and it will end in mystery,
but what a savage
and beautiful country
lies in between.

DIANE ACKERMAN, B.1948

Among the mind's powers is one that comes of itself to many children and artists. It need not be lost, to the end of our days, by anyone who has ever had it. This is the power of taking delight in a thing, or rather in anything, not as a means to some other end but just because it is what it is. A child in the full health of his mind will put his hand flat on the summer turf, feel it, and give a little shiver of private glee at the elastic firmness of the globe.

CHARLES EDWARD MONTAGUE (1867-1928)

$\mathcal{N}$o words can describe
the spiritual thrill
and feeling of expectancy
and longing which
the beauty of a rose-coloured sky
at dawn can provoke.

MARY O'HARA

I don't want to get to the end of my life and find that I just lived the length of it. I want to have lived the width of it as well.

DIANE ACKERMAN, B. 1948

Surely the strange beauty of the world must somewhere rest on pure joy!

LOUISE BOGAN (1897-1970)

Don't ever save anything for a special occasion. Being alive is the special occasion.

AUTHOR UNKNOWN

Happiness is when everyday things shine like gold.

PAM BROWN (1928-2014)

Wear flowers
in your hair,
Splash in puddles,
Laugh with the wind,
Be happy!
Make happiness
your purpose in life.

STUART & LINDA MACFARLANE

If you
get a chance,
take it.
If it changes
your life,
let it.

HARVEY MACKAY, B. 1932

*Y*ou do not need to leave your room... Remain sitting at your table and listen. Do not even listen, simply wait. Do not even wait, be still and solitary. The world will freely offer itself to you to be unmasked. It has no choice. It will roll in ecstasy at your feet.

FRANZ KAFKA (1883-1924)

Don't ask what the world needs. Ask what makes you come alive, and go do it. Because what the world needs is more people who have life..

HOWARD THURMAN

Life is short,
break the rules,
forgive quickly,
kiss slowly,
love truly,
laugh uncontrollably
and never regret anything
that made you smile.

MARK TWAIN (1835-1910)

*I'm filled with joy
when the day dawns
quietly
over the roof of the sky.*

ESKIMO LOVE SONG

Every morning,
when we wake up,
we have twenty-four brand-new hours
to live.

THICH NHAT HANH, B. 1926

*I*t is eternity now.
I am in the midst of it.
It is about me in the sunshine;
I am in it, as the butterfly floats
in the light-laden air.
Nothing has to come;
it is now.
Now is eternity.

RICHARD JEFFERIES (1848-1887)

*Each day the first day:
Each day a life.*

DAG HAMMARSKJÖLD (1905-1961)

O Wonderful,
wonderful,
and most wonderful
wonderful,
and yet again
wonderful,
and after that out of all
whooping!

WILLIAM SHAKESPEARE (1564-1616)